Dedicated to
Charlie Van Loon
May he know Jesus
at a very young age
and follow Him
all the days of his life.

# Acknowledgments

Gabby and Abby are ever grateful to Linda L. Keating
for her adoration for the LORD and His Word
and editing to make this book as close to perfect
as we can get!

# Tech support

Special gratitude to Chris Babb
for his tech support to make
Gabby and Abby's adventure
a great little children's book.

# Forward

I think the most difficult thing for me to do in
my walk with God is to hold my tongue. I try to be
an encourager everywhere I go.  The most challenging
place to hold my tongue is at home with the people
who I love most but they also test me the most.
I hope this book will be not only a helping tool
to speak better words to others as we read it to our kids,
but to be convicted ourselves.

Gabby is a rare bird
who has the gift of gab.

"Let the words of my mouth
and the meditation of my heart
be acceptable in thy sight,
O Jehovah,
my rock, and
my redeemer."
Psalm 19:14

1

Every word she speaks
is never dry nor drab.

2

"A person finds joy in giving an apt reply-
and how good is a timely word." Proverbs 15:23

# 3    She's free as a bird and happy as a lark!

"Look at the birds of the air;
they neither sow nor reap
nor gather into barns,
and yet your heavenly Father
feeds them.
Are you not of more value than they?"
Matthew 6:26

She encourages everyone with her cheerful spark!

"A merry heart does good like a medicine,
but a broken spirit dries the bones." Proverbs 17:22

5

Gabby has one friend
who is faithful as the sun.

"Many a man proclaims his own loyalty and goodness,
but who can find a faithful and trustworthy man?"  Proverbs 20:6

9

and night owls too!

"A friend loves at all times..."
Proverbs 17:17a

He went on a wild goose chase,
and disappeared like the dodo.

"I have observed everything
going on under the sun,
and really,
it is all meaningless-
like chasing after the wind."
Ecclesiastes 1:14

"Many women do noble things,
but you surpass them all.
Charm is deceptive, and beauty is fleeting;
but a woman who fears the LORD is to be praised.
Honor her for all that her hands have done,
and let her works bring praise at the city gate."
Proverbs 31:29-31

12

Under the wings of her mom,
they work hard to get by.

And one day Gabby will spread her wings and fly.

13

"Train up a child in the way he should go;
even when he is old he will not depart from it."
Proverbs 22:6

14

Her Nana and Papa
live up the path
as far as a crows fly,

"Incline your ear,
and hear the words of the wise,
and apply your heart to my knowledge."
Proverbs 22:17

"For if we are out of our mind, it is for God;
if we are in our right mind, it is for you."
2 Corinthians 5:13

15

Silly aunt Lulu crazy as a loon,
has bats in the belfry.

Her Nana is silly as a goose,
and her Papa is bald as a coot,

"Gray hair is a crown of glory;
it is gained by living a godly life."
Proverbs 16:31

16

But when they're all together,
their cackles are a crazy hoot!

"A cheerful heart is good medicine,
but a broken spirit saps a person's strength."
Proverbs 17:22

17

Nana is no spring chicken,
but she can cook as easy as duck soup.

"For I can do everything through Christ,
who gives me strength."
Philippians 4:13

18

If Papa is wise as an owl,
he'll eat crow before he spends the
night in the coop!

"If you punish a mocker,
the simpleminded will learn a lesson;
if you correct the wise,
they will be all the wiser."
Proverbs 19:25

19

And they love to talk turkey
while hanging with the folks.

"The lips of the wise give good advice;
the heart of a fool has none to give."
Proverbs 15:7

Gabby's favorite past time is
flapping with her best friend.

"The righteous choose their friends carefully,
but the way of the wicked leads them astray."
Proverbs 12:26

22

They both are different and find it hard to blend.

"Be completely humble and gentle; be patient, bearing
with one another in love."
Ephesians 4:2

23

Abby is sometimes unavailable to exchange words.

"Timely advice is lovely,
like golden apples in a silver
basket."
Proverbs 25:11

24

**25**

Gabby gets impatient
and says,
"this is for the birds."

"Above all else,
guard your heart,
for everything you do
flows from it."
Proverbs 4:23

Close friends are as scarce as a hen's teeth
and hard to find.

"A man of many companions may come to ruin,
but there is a friend who sticks closer than a brother."
Proverbs 18:24

26

Gabby's sure to have more friends
and Abby won't mind.

"There's no fear in love.
But perfect love
drives out fear,
because fear has to do
 with punishment.
 The one who
fears is not
made perfect in love.
We love because
he first loved us."
1 John 18, 19

27

"Thus says the LORD, your Redeemer, the Holy One of Israel;
'I am the LORD your God who teaches you to profit,
who leads you in the way you should go."
Isaiah 48:17

28

It was time
to take a bird's eye view
to see whether,

birds of a feather flock together.

29

"Do not be deceived, 'Bad company ruins good morals.'"
1st Corinthians 15:33

Gabby spotted a gaggle of geese
babbling about this and that.

"So get rid of all evil behavior.
Be done with deceit, hypocrisy,
jealousy, and all unkind speech."
1 Peter 2:1

30

They played chicken
and invited her to come and chat.

"So stop telling lies.
Let us tell our neighbors the truth,
for we are all parts of the same body."
Ephesians 4:25

31

They urged her to say,
"Abby's an ugly duckling, and morbidly plain."

32

"Gentle words are a tree of life;
a deceitful tongue crushes the spirit."
Proverbs 15:4

"A little bird told me,"
said one goose,
"Abby's a bird brain!"

"When there are many words,
transgression is unavoidable,
But he who restrains his lips is wise."
Proverbs 10:19

33

The words were harmful
and Gabby was mad!

"A gentle answer deflects anger,
but harsh words make tempers flare."
Proverbs 15:1

34

No one was going to make her best friend sad.

"Love is patient,
love is kind.
It does not envy,
it does not boast,
it is not proud.
It does not
dishonor others,
it is not self-seeking,
it is not
easily angered,
it keeps no record
of wrongs.
Love does not
delight in evil,
but rejoices with the truth.
It always protects,
always trusts,
always hopes,
always perseveres.
Love never fails."
1 Corinthians
13:4-8

35

She was no chicken-livered chick, she refused to chicken-out!

"The LORD detests the thoughts of the wicked, but gracious words are pure in His sight."
Proverbs 15:26

36

She marched on over as mad
as a wet hen and without a doubt.

37

"Fools give full vent to their rage,
but the wise bring calm in the end."
Proverbs 29:11

# Gabby's goosebumps swelled
## to hear all that slander!

"Whoever goes about slandering reveals secrets;
therefore do not associate with a simple babbler."
Proverbs 20:19

38

What's good for the goose,
is good for the gander.

"Do not repay evil for evil.
Do not retaliate with insults
when people insult you.
Instead, pay them back with a blessing.
That is what God has called you to do,
and He will bless you for it."
1 Peter 3:9

39

Abby's not like that,
I want you to know!

40

"A fool is quick-tempered,
but a wise person stays calm when insulted."
Proverbs 12:16

She talked until she was hoarse as a crow.

"Finally, brothers, whatever is true,
whatever is honorable, whatever is just,
whatever is pure, whatever is lovely,
whatever is commendable,
if there is any excellence,
if there is anything worthy of praise,
think about these things."
Philippians 4:8

41

Instead of squawking like a chicken
with it's head cut off,

"But love your enemies,
do good to them,
and lend to them without expecting anything back.
Then your reward will be great, and
you will be children of the Most High,
because He is kind to those who are
ungrateful and wicked."
Luke 6:35

42

Gabby made a choice to
defend with kind words
instead of scoff.

"Death and life are in the power of the tongue,
and those who love it will eat its fruits."
Proverbs 18:21

43

She used words that were loving but firm.

"Instead, speaking the truth in love,
we will grow to become in every respect the
mature body of Him who is the head, that is, Christ."
Ephesians 4:15

44

And you should have seen them
squirm like a worm.

"Do to others
as you would have them
do to you."
Luke 6:31

I'll side with my friend
because she will not be a sitting duck.

"Two are better than one,
because they have a good return
for their work;
If one falls down, his friend can help him up."
Ecclesiastes 4:9, 10

46

It doesn't matter if we're neither fish nor foul or if we get stuck.

47

"Dear friends, let us love one another, for love comes from God."
1 John 4:7

Like a feather in one's cap,
Abby was a friend to honor
and stick by.

"Light in a messenger's eyes brings joy to the heart,
and good news gives health to the bones."
Proverbs 15:30

48

"You are the people of God;
He loved you and chose you for His own.
So then, you must clothe yourselves with
compassion, kindness, humility, gentleness, and patience.
Be tolerant with one another and forgive
one another whenever
any of you have a complaint
against someone else.
You must forgive one another
just as the LORD has forgiven you.
And to all these qualities
add love, which binds all things
together in perfect unity.
Colossians 3:12-14

49

Everyone needs a friend who's an awesome ally.

50

You can ruffle Gabby's feathers,
but she's not alone.

"Let the morning bring me word
of your unfailing love."
Psalm 143:8

51

Defending a friend
and speaking kind words,
is killing two birds with one stone.

"Above all, love each other deeply,
because love covers a multitude of sins."
1 Peter 4:8

Like water off a ducks back,
they didn't let it sink in.

"This is what the LORD says:
'Cursed is the one who trusts in man,
who depends on flesh for his strength
and whose heart turns away
from the LORD.'"
Jeremiah 17:5

52

"This is what the LORD requires of you;
Do justice, love kindness, and walk
humbly with your God."
Micah 6:8

53    Because Gabby and Abby
are each other's best friend.

"Then Peter opened his mouth, and said,
'Of a truth I perceive
 that God is no respecter of
persons; But in every nation
he that fears him,
and works righteousness,
 is accepted with him.'"
Acts 10:34, 35

Gabby is loyal to Abby
and they have no pecking order,

54

"He who walks with the wise
grows wise,
but a companion of fools
suffers harm."
Proverbs 13:20

They're equal and respect one another's border.

56

"Love must be sincere.
Hate what is evil;
cling to what is good.
Be devoted to one another in love.
Honor one another above yourselves.
Never be lacking in zeal,
but keep your spiritual fervor,
serving the LORD.
Be joyful in hope,
patient in affliction,
faithful in prayer.
Share with the LORD's people
who are in need.
Practice hospitality. Bless those who
persecute you; bless and do not curse.
Rejoice with those who rejoice;
mourn with those who mourn.
Live in harmony with one another."
Romans 12:9–16

As graceful as a swan,
they went home in a rush!

Because a bird in one hand
is better than two in the bush.

"Are not two sparrows sold for a penny?
Yet not one of them will fall to the ground outside
your Father's care.  And even the very hairs of your head
are all numbered.  So don't be afraid;
you are worth more than many sparrows."
Matthew 10:29-31

57

" For where two or more are gathered
in My name, I am there."
Matthew 18:20

Gabby and Abby
pray together this verse;
Dear LORD,
Put a guard over my mouth
so that I may not sin against you!
In Jesus name.
Amen

58

# Prayer for me

Heavenly Father, I thank you for my friend.
I thank You for Jesus who is my best friend first because
He loves me first and more than I know.
I thank You Father for sending Jesus to die
for me and take my place for all the things I think,
say, and do that does not please You.
Help me with my words to those who are not nice to me.
I believe you can help by living inside my heart. Come into my heart now.
In Jesus name, Amen

# Gabby's Daily Prayer

"Set a guard over my
mouth, LORD;
keep watch over the door
of my lips."
Psalm 141:3

# Gabby's MO

"Love must be sincere. Hate what is evil; cling to what is good.
Be devoted to one another in love. Honor one another above yourselves.
Never be lacking in zeal, but keep your spiritual fervor, serving the LORD.
Be joyful in hope, patient in affliction, faithful in prayer.
Share with the LORD's people who are in need. Practice hospitality.
Bless those who persecute you; bless and do not curse.
Rejoice with those who rejoice;
mourn with those who mourn.
Live in harmony with one another."
Romans 12:9–16

# Whatever...

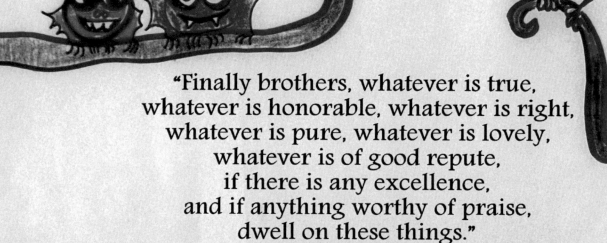

"Finally brothers, whatever is true,
whatever is honorable, whatever is right,
whatever is pure, whatever is lovely,
whatever is of good repute,
if there is any excellence,
and if anything worthy of praise,
dwell on these things."
Philippians 4:8

Edythe lives in
Temecula, California.
She loves writing
books that honor
her Lord and Savior
Jesus Christ.
She has 3 sons
Matthew, John Luke,
and Seth Mark, and
she has a daugher-in-law
Leah who gave her
the cutest grandson,
Charlie.

Photo courtesy
Seth Abell
July 2018

John Abell
is pursuing a hobby/career
as a writer and illustrator.
He has drawn several birds for
Gabby Gabby.
Many thanks for his time and
dedication in helping to create
colorful, expression filled, and
exciting images for
Gabby Gabby. He is also credited for
editing parts of the book.
I'm grateful for his help in making
Gabby Gabby a reality.

"With the tongue we praise our Lord and Father,
and with it we curse human beings,
who have been made in God's likeness.
Out of the same mouth come praise and cursing.
My brothers and sisters this should not be."
James 3:9,10